CAPUCHIN MONKEY

The complete guide to raising, caring for, and enjoying this intelligent and playful primate

JEROME BOUCHARD

1

Table of Contents

CHAPTER ONE
INTRODUCTION TO CAPUCHIN MONKEYS

Capuchin monkeys are one of the most well-known and captivating species within the primate family. Renowned for their intelligence and social behaviors, they are a popular subject of study in both the animal care and research communities. As a type of New World monkey, capuchins are native to the tropical forests of Central and South America. The name "capuchin" is derived from the Italian word *"capuccini"*, referring to the Capuchin friars, due to the distinctive color and shape of the monkeys' fur, which resembles the hooded habits worn by these monks. These monkeys belong to the genus *Cebus*, which encompasses several species, all sharing certain common traits but differing in size, appearance, and behavior.

Capuchins are most famous for their dexterity and cognitive capabilities, which rival those of some great apes. With a strong grip and excellent hand-eye coordination, they can manipulate objects with remarkable precision. They are also known for their social intelligence, forming complex social structures and communicating in sophisticated ways. This combination of traits makes them stand out in the animal kingdom, particularly among the monkeys. Their role in the ecosystem is also important, as they contribute to seed dispersal and help maintain the balance of their forest environments.

The World of Capuchins: Species Overview

There are two main species of capuchin monkeys, the *Cebus* and *Sapajus* genera. Historically, these species were grouped together under the genus

Cebus, but research has since separated them into two distinct groups based on subtle but significant differences in their behavior, anatomy, and genetics. The *Cebus* genus includes the white-faced capuchin (*Cebus capucinus*) and the Panama capuchin (*Cebus imitator*), among others. These monkeys are generally known for their lighter-colored fur, with the white-faced capuchin being especially famous for its distinct coloration and use in popular media.

On the other hand, the *Sapajus* genus, often referred to as the "tufted capuchins," includes species like the *Sapajus apella*, known as the brown capuchin, and the *Sapajus libidinosus*. These species tend to be slightly larger and have darker fur with more pronounced tufts on their heads, making them more easily distinguishable from their *Cebus* counterparts. While both genera share similar behavioral traits, such as their tool-using abilities and social complexity, the physical

and behavioral differences are considerable enough to warrant separate classification.

Capuchin monkeys are highly adaptable and can be found in a variety of habitats, from the rainforests of the Amazon basin to the dry forests of northeastern Brazil. They thrive in the dense canopies of these tropical environments, where they form large, tightly-knit social groups that are often led by an alpha male. These groups can range in size from 10 to 40 individuals, with an intricate social structure that dictates behavior within the group. Capuchins are omnivorous, foraging for a wide variety of foods, including fruits, insects, small vertebrates, and even the occasional bird egg. Their remarkable ability to use tools, such as rocks to crack open nuts or sticks to extract insects from tree bark, sets them apart from many other primates and highlights their advanced cognitive abilities.

Natural Habitat and Behavior in the Wild

Capuchins primarily inhabit tropical and subtropical forests, although some species can also be found in more arid regions. These monkeys are most active during the day, foraging for food and engaging in social activities within their troop. They are excellent climbers, spending much of their time in the trees, where they forage for fruits, nuts, seeds, and invertebrates. Their ability to navigate through the treetops with agility and precision is one of the key factors that helps them survive in their natural habitats. Capuchins are also known to be opportunistic feeders, often hunting or scavenging for food wherever they can find it.

The behavior of capuchins is deeply social, and their troop dynamics are complex. They have been observed to engage in a wide variety of social behaviors, from grooming to play, and they communicate using a range of vocalizations, facial

expressions, and body language. Group cohesion is essential for their survival, as capuchins rely on cooperation to protect each other from predators and to secure food sources. These monkeys are also highly territorial and will fiercely defend their home range from other troops, especially when food resources are scarce.

Capuchins are known for their high intelligence, and much of their behavior reflects their ability to solve problems and use tools. One of the most famous examples of their tool use is their ability to crack open hard-shelled nuts using rocks or other hard objects. They have also been seen using sticks to fish for termites or to extract other small animals from crevices in trees. This ability to innovate and adapt their behavior to changing circumstances has made capuchins a subject of much interest to scientists studying animal cognition.

In conclusion, capuchin monkeys are fascinating creatures, known for their intelligence, complex social behavior, and adaptability. While they can make engaging and affectionate pets, they require a significant commitment to meet their physical, social, and emotional needs. Understanding the challenges and responsibilities involved in caring for these animals is essential for anyone considering them as pets.

CHAPTER TWO

UNDERSTANDING CAPUCHIN BEHAVIOR AND TRAITS

Capuchin monkeys are fascinating creatures that exhibit a variety of behavioral traits and characteristics. As one of the most intelligent and socially complex species of New World monkeys, understanding their behavior and traits is essential for anyone studying or caring for them. From their physical attributes to their cognitive abilities and intricate social lives, capuchins are truly remarkable animals. In this section, we will explore their physical characteristics, intelligence and problem-solving abilities, and social structure, offering insights into what makes them unique.

Physical Characteristics: Size, Coat, and Features

Capuchin monkeys are medium-sized primates with some distinct physical features that set them apart from other species. Adult capuchins typically weigh between 4 and 10 pounds (1.8 to 4.5 kg), with females generally being smaller than males. They have a body length ranging from 16 to 24 inches (40 to 60 cm), not including the tail, which is prehensile and adds an additional 16 to 24 inches (40 to 60 cm) to their overall length. Their prehensile tail is one of the most notable characteristics, as it functions like a fifth limb, enabling them to grasp branches with remarkable dexterity and stability. This tail is essential for their arboreal lifestyle, allowing them to move through trees with agility and ease.

Capuchins' fur is typically short to medium in length, with the color varying depending on the species. For example, the white-faced capuchin

(*Cebus capucinus*) has a lighter coat with a distinct white or cream-colored face, while the brown capuchin (*Sapajus apella*) has darker fur with slight tufts on its head. Their fur is dense and soft, providing some insulation against their environment. One of the key features of capuchins is their face, which is expressive and human-like in many ways. Their facial features, such as their large eyes and expressive brows, allow for a wide range of communication, not only with other capuchins but also with humans.

Intelligence and Problem-Solving Abilities

Capuchin monkeys are widely regarded for their exceptional intelligence, which is a major factor in their ability to adapt to various environments and solve complex problems. Their cognitive abilities are particularly evident in their tool use, which is considered one of the most advanced among non-human primates. Capuchins are known to use rocks, sticks, and other objects to access food, such as cracking open nuts, breaking shells, or extracting insects from crevices. Their ability to use tools in a variety of ways demonstrates their capacity for innovation, problem-solving, and foresight.

Studies have shown that capuchins can plan and execute tasks that require a sequence of actions, showcasing their understanding of cause and effect. For example, they might use one object to retrieve another, such as using a stick to get to a treat that is out of reach. This behavior is indicative of advanced cognitive processing, and it is believed that capuchins, like other primates, have the ability to learn by observation, further enhancing their problem-solving capabilities. This learning by observation allows them to pass on knowledge within their social groups, which is essential for survival in the wild.

Moreover, capuchins have demonstrated the ability to understand social cues and use them to their advantage, which reflects their high level of intelligence. They can recognize individuals within their group, establish hierarchies, and even cooperate with others to achieve goals. They also exhibit a level of empathy, as they have been observed sharing food with others in their group, particularly with relatives or close companions. This social intelligence plays a critical role in their survival, as their ability to cooperate and work together helps them locate food and protect each other from predators.

Social Structure and Emotional Needs

Capuchins are highly social animals, living in large, complex groups that range from 10 to 40 individuals. Within these groups, there is a well-defined social structure, often headed by an alpha male, although females also play an important role in the group's dynamics. The social hierarchy is established through both aggression and affiliative behaviors, with individuals vying for dominance but also forming bonds with others through grooming and play. These social bonds are crucial for the emotional well-being of capuchins, as they provide a sense of security and stability within the group.

The emotional needs of capuchins are deeply connected to their social interactions. They form close, lasting relationships with other group members, especially with their mothers, siblings, and close companions. Capuchins are known to engage in grooming, a behavior that serves not only to keep their fur clean but also to strengthen social ties. Grooming is a form of bonding and helps to reduce stress and tension within the group. This social grooming is often reciprocated, with individuals grooming each other to reinforce their relationships and maintain harmony within the troop.

Capuchins also engage in a variety of other social behaviors, including play, which is vital for their emotional development, especially in younger individuals. Play often involves chasing, wrestling, and mock fighting, which helps them learn important social skills, such as cooperation, conflict resolution, and the establishment of dominance. These playful interactions are important not just for physical development but also for the emotional health of capuchins, as they provide an outlet for energy and promote group cohesion.

In the wild, the emotional well-being of capuchins is closely linked to their environment and the availability of resources. They are highly territorial and will defend their home range from other troops. Their territorial behavior is partly driven by the need to secure access to food and shelter but also by the desire to protect their social structure. In captivity, however, capuchins may experience stress if their social needs are not met. Without the presence of other capuchins, or without the opportunity to engage in natural social behaviors, they can become anxious, depressed, or exhibit signs of behavioral problems. This makes it crucial for pet owners or caregivers to understand the emotional and social needs of capuchins and to provide an environment that allows them to interact, play, and communicate with others of their kind.

In conclusion, understanding the behavior and traits of capuchin monkeys is essential for appreciating their complexity as both wild animals and, in some cases, exotic pets. Their physical characteristics, particularly their dexterous tails and expressive faces, help them navigate their environments and communicate with one another. Their intelligence and problem-solving abilities set them apart from many other animals, allowing them to adapt to challenges and innovate in their foraging and social behaviors. Lastly, their intricate social structures and deep emotional needs highlight the importance of maintaining strong relationships within their groups, both in the wild and in captivity. Recognizing these aspects of capuchin behavior is essential for anyone seeking to understand or care for these remarkable primates.

CHAPTER THREE
PREPARING FOR A
CAPUCHIN MONKEY

Capuchin monkeys are intelligent, social, and active animals that require significant commitment and attention from their owners. Preparing to bring a capuchin monkey into your home is not a decision to be taken lightly. These primates have specialized needs, and the responsibility of caring for them is complex, involving careful planning and the fulfillment of legal, ethical, and practical requirements. In this section, we will discuss the legal and ethical considerations of owning a capuchin monkey, how to find a reputable breeder or rescue, and the essential supplies and home preparations needed to ensure your new companion's health and happiness.

Legal and Ethical Considerations of Ownership

Before acquiring a capuchin monkey, the first and most important step is understanding the legal and ethical considerations associated with owning an exotic pet. In many regions, owning a capuchin monkey is regulated or outright prohibited. These laws are in place to protect both the welfare of the animal and public safety, as primates are not domesticated and can present significant challenges when kept as pets. It's crucial to research your local laws and regulations regarding exotic pet ownership, as they can vary greatly depending on your country, state, or municipality.

In some places, a special permit or license may be required to own a capuchin monkey, and you may need to prove that you have the resources, experience, and knowledge to care for such an animal. Be sure to consult local wildlife authorities or animal control to get up-to-date information on the legal requirements in your area. Additionally, it's important to be aware of any restrictions or regulations that may govern the importation or breeding of exotic animals.

From an ethical standpoint, owning a capuchin monkey raises significant concerns. These animals are highly intelligent, social creatures that thrive in the wild in complex social structures. Keeping a capuchin as a pet means removing it from its natural habitat, where it plays an essential role in its ecosystem. The ethics of keeping a capuchin monkey in captivity are debated by animal welfare experts, who argue that primates require the stimulation, social interaction, and natural environment that captivity often cannot provide. Potential owners must carefully weigh these ethical concerns and consider whether they can provide the necessary environment to meet the monkey's physical and emotional needs.

Finding a Reputable Breeder or Rescue

Once you have determined that owning a capuchin monkey is legal and ethical in your area, the next step is to find a reputable source for acquiring one. Whether you decide to adopt from a rescue organization or purchase from a breeder, ensuring that the monkey has been raised in a responsible and humane manner is critical to its long-term well-being.

Finding a reputable breeder is a challenging task, as there are unfortunately some breeders who prioritize profit over the welfare of the animals they sell. A responsible breeder will raise the monkeys in a clean, safe environment, providing them with socialization, enrichment, and proper veterinary care from an early age. Reputable breeders typically focus on breeding monkeys with good temperaments and avoid inbreeding or unethical practices that could harm the animals' health.

It's essential to ask the breeder for detailed information about the animal's lineage, health history, and socialization experiences. A responsible breeder will be transparent about the monkey's background and will provide you with any necessary documentation, including vaccination records and health clearances. Additionally, they should be willing to show you the conditions in which the monkeys are raised, so you can ensure that they are given proper care and attention before they are sold.

Alternatively, adopting from a reputable animal rescue organization can be an excellent option, especially if you are looking to provide a home for a capuchin in need. Rescue organizations often take in monkeys that have been relinquished by previous owners or rescued from illegal trafficking. By adopting from a rescue, you can provide a loving home to a capuchin that may have experienced trauma or neglect in the past. However, rescues typically require potential adopters to meet stringent criteria to ensure that the animal will be placed in a suitable environment. This can include home visits, interviews, and a thorough screening process to assess your ability to care for the animal.

Regardless of whether you choose to purchase from a breeder or adopt from a rescue, always be cautious and do your due diligence. Avoid purchasing capuchin monkeys from pet stores, online marketplaces, or individuals who are not fully transparent about the animal's background. In addition, avoid breeders or rescues that appear to be more focused on making a sale than on ensuring the welfare of the animals.

Initial Supplies and Home Preparations

Proper preparation for a capuchin monkey involves not only finding a reputable source for the animal but also ensuring that your home is ready to meet the physical, emotional, and social needs of the monkey. Capuchins require an environment that is safe, stimulating, and enriched, as well as plenty of space for exercise and mental engagement.

The first step in preparing your home is to create a suitable living space for the monkey. Capuchins are arboreal creatures, meaning they spend a significant amount of time in the trees in the wild. As a result, they need a large enclosure that mimics their natural environment as closely as possible. The enclosure should be spacious enough for the monkey to move around freely and should include various levels, platforms, and ropes or branches for climbing. These structures will allow your capuchin to exercise, explore, and satisfy its natural instincts to climb and leap. A secure, escape-proof enclosure is a must, as capuchins are agile and can easily escape from enclosures that are not properly secured.

In addition to an enclosure, you will need to provide a variety of other supplies to ensure your capuchin's well-being. This includes bedding material, such as soft towels, blankets, or a non-toxic mulch that provides comfort and insulation. You'll also need food and water dishes, as well as a variety of stimulating toys and enrichment items. Capuchins are highly intelligent and need mental stimulation to avoid boredom and behavioral problems. Puzzle feeders, ropes, mirrors, and objects that encourage foraging are excellent ways to engage your capuchin's mind and promote natural behaviors.

You will also need to prepare your home to accommodate the social and emotional needs of the capuchin monkey. Capuchins are highly social animals, so they require constant companionship and interaction, whether with other monkeys or humans. Consider how much time you can devote to interacting with your monkey each day. If you plan to keep only one capuchin, ensure that you can offer enough attention and enrichment to fulfill its social needs. If possible, consider the option of adopting a second monkey to prevent loneliness and boredom.

Finally, capuchins require specialized veterinary care, so it is essential to find a veterinarian who is experienced in treating primates. Regular check-ups, vaccinations, and preventative health care will be necessary to maintain your monkey's health. This includes ensuring that the monkey is on a balanced diet of fresh fruits, vegetables, and protein, as well as supplements to support its long-term health. Providing regular opportunities for exercise, social interaction, and mental stimulation is also crucial for your capuchin's overall well-being.

In conclusion, preparing for a capuchin monkey involves careful consideration of legal, ethical, and practical aspects. Understanding the laws in your area, choosing a reputable source for your monkey, and preparing your home with the necessary supplies and environment are all essential steps in ensuring that your capuchin has a happy, healthy life. It's a significant commitment that requires a great deal of responsibility, but with proper preparation and dedication, you can provide a fulfilling and enriching life for your capuchin monkey.

CHAPTER FOUR

CREATING THE IDEAL HABITAT

Creating the ideal habitat for a capuchin monkey is an essential aspect of ensuring its physical and emotional well-being. These intelligent and social animals require an environment that caters to their complex needs for exercise, mental stimulation, social interaction, and safety. A well-designed habitat allows your capuchin to thrive, both physically and mentally, by providing sufficient space, opportunities for climbing, and enrichment. This section will discuss the indoor and outdoor enclosure requirements for capuchins, enrichment accessories that can enhance their habitat, and how to ensure safety and security within their living environment.

Indoor and Outdoor Enclosure Requirements

The first step in creating a suitable habitat for a capuchin monkey is to design an enclosure that allows them to express their natural behaviors. Since capuchins are arboreal by nature, they spend a lot of time in the trees, using their agility to climb, swing, and leap. Therefore, both indoor and outdoor enclosures should be spacious enough to accommodate these behaviors.

Indoor Enclosure Requirements: For indoor enclosures, size is of utmost importance. A capuchin monkey requires a large, secure space where it can move freely. The enclosure should be at least 8-10 feet tall, with multiple levels or platforms for climbing. While there is no strict minimum size requirement, a space of around 10 feet by 10 feet or larger would be ideal for one monkey. The enclosure should include sturdy materials, such as metal or strong wire mesh, to prevent escapes. Capuchins are known for their strength and agility, so the wire should be strong enough to withstand their attempts to climb or chew through it.

The indoor habitat should provide a variety of climbing opportunities. Install ropes, branches, or ladders to mimic a natural environment. Capuchins are naturally curious, and providing them with objects to manipulate, explore, and climb will keep them engaged. It is important to create a safe and secure environment, so ensure that there are no gaps or weak points in the structure where the monkey could escape or become injured. The flooring should be made of non-toxic materials that are easy to clean, such as durable rubber mats or tiles.

Outdoor Enclosure Requirements: Outdoor enclosures are equally important, particularly if you live in an area with a suitable climate for outdoor living. Outdoor spaces offer your capuchin monkey the opportunity to enjoy fresh air, sunlight, and a more natural setting. However, outdoor enclosures must be just as secure and safe as indoor ones to prevent escape or injury.

The size of the outdoor enclosure should be large enough to give the monkey ample space to move and explore. A space of at least 12 feet by 12 feet, with a height of 10 feet or more, is ideal. Just like with the indoor enclosure, the walls should be constructed of strong, chew-resistant materials. If the enclosure has a roof, it should be made of sturdy wire mesh to prevent the monkey from climbing over. The enclosure should be securely fenced on all sides, with an underground barrier if necessary, to prevent the monkey from digging under the fence.

Outdoor enclosures should also be designed to provide enrichment and comfort. The enclosure can include trees or tall shrubs, climbing platforms, and shelters that allow the monkey to rest in a shaded or sheltered area. A variety of natural textures and surfaces, such as branches, rocks, or sand, can add to the environmental complexity. Outdoor spaces should be protected from extreme weather conditions, such as intense heat, heavy rain, or cold, to ensure the monkey's comfort and safety. Therefore, it is important to provide adequate shelter where the capuchin can retreat if needed.

Enrichment Accessories: Climbing Structures and Toys

Capuchin monkeys are incredibly intelligent and active animals that require constant mental and physical stimulation. Without sufficient enrichment, they can develop boredom, anxiety, and destructive behaviors. Therefore, providing climbing structures and toys within their enclosure is essential for their well-being.

Climbing Structures: As primarily arboreal animals, capuchins thrive in environments that allow them to climb, leap, and explore. Adding climbing structures such as ropes, ladders, ramps, and shelves in the enclosure is key to encouraging these natural behaviors. Sturdy ropes made of hemp or sisal are excellent choices for climbing, as capuchins enjoy swinging and using them to maneuver across their habitat. Branches, whether natural or artificial, should be placed at varying heights and angles to simulate a more natural, dynamic environment. This allows the monkey to explore different levels and engage in physical exercise.

Additionally, incorporating platforms or small elevated areas where the capuchin can rest, observe its surroundings, or eat is important for providing variety and comfort. These elevated spots are also essential for encouraging the monkey to feel safe and secure, as they often enjoy being able to observe their environment from a height. Branches with varying textures will encourage the monkey to grasp and manipulate them, supporting its natural climbing and foraging instincts.

Toys and Enrichment Items: Toys are another critical aspect of enrichment for capuchins. Since these monkeys are highly intelligent, interactive toys can help stimulate their problem-solving abilities and prevent boredom. Puzzle feeders, for example, challenge the capuchin to figure out how to retrieve food, which mimics foraging behaviors in the wild. These toys not only provide mental stimulation but also reward the monkey for using its intelligence, creating a sense of accomplishment.

Other toys that can be added to the enclosure include hanging objects like mirrors, balls, and various textures that the monkey can manipulate. Chew toys made from natural materials, such as wood or coconut, are also beneficial, as capuchins love to chew and gnaw on objects. Safe, non-toxic toys can help fulfill their need to explore and investigate objects. Rotate the toys and enrichment items regularly to keep the capuchin monkey engaged, as they can become bored with the same items over time.

Interactive toys like ropes, swings, and hanging treats can encourage physical activity and play. These items not only provide fun but also help to maintain the monkey's physical health by encouraging it to move and exercise regularly. Enrichment for capuchins should be diverse and include toys that challenge both their physical and mental faculties.

Ensuring Safety and Security in the Environment

Creating a safe and secure environment for a capuchin monkey is of paramount importance. These monkeys are incredibly agile and strong, which means that any enclosure needs to be carefully constructed to prevent escape and protect the monkey from harm. Regular checks for weaknesses in the enclosure, such as gaps in the wire or loose panels, are necessary to ensure the security of the environment.

Escape-Proofing the Enclosure: Capuchins are clever and capable of manipulating their environment, so an escape-proof enclosure is crucial. Ensure that all openings are small enough that the monkey cannot squeeze through, and use thick, chew-resistant materials for the walls and bars. The enclosure should be secured with strong locks, as capuchins are dexterous and can figure out how to open simple latches. For outdoor enclosures, make sure there is an underground barrier to prevent digging and escaping.

Preventing Injury: The enclosure should also be designed to prevent injury. Sharp objects, exposed nails, or corners where the monkey could hurt itself should be avoided. Any materials used in the construction of climbing structures or toys should be non-toxic and safe for chewing. Additionally, ensure that the enclosure provides adequate shelter from extreme weather and temperature conditions, as capuchins are sensitive to environmental changes.

Regular Maintenance and Monitoring: Safety in the habitat doesn't stop once the enclosure is set up. Regular maintenance is essential to keep the environment secure and in good condition. Inspect the structure frequently for wear and tear, check for any escape routes, and ensure that all enrichment items are safe and in working order. Keeping the enclosure clean and free of waste is also important for the monkey's health. A routine cleaning schedule should be established, using safe, non-toxic cleaning products that will not harm the monkey.

In conclusion, creating the ideal habitat for a capuchin monkey requires careful planning and attention to detail. By designing spacious indoor and outdoor enclosures that allow for natural climbing and exploration, providing stimulating toys and enrichment, and ensuring safety and security, you can create an environment that supports your capuchin's physical, mental, and emotional health. This level of care and preparation will contribute to a fulfilling and enriched life for your monkey, helping it to thrive in its home.

CHAPTER FIVE
FEEDING AND NUTRITION

Proper feeding and nutrition are vital to the health and well-being of capuchin monkeys. These intelligent primates have complex dietary needs that must be met to ensure they thrive in both captivity and the wild. In their natural habitats, capuchins are omnivores, foraging for a wide variety of foods such as fruits, insects, small animals, nuts, and seeds. When keeping capuchin monkeys as pets, it is crucial to replicate this balanced diet as closely as possible, offering a mix of fresh fruits, vegetables, proteins, and other necessary nutrients while avoiding foods that could be harmful or cause nutritional imbalances. Understanding these dietary needs, choosing safe foods, and knowing what to avoid can ensure that your capuchin remains healthy, active, and happy.

Understanding Capuchin Dietary Needs

Capuchin monkeys have evolved as omnivores, meaning they consume a diverse range of plant and animal-based foods. In the wild, their diet varies depending on seasonal availability and their immediate environment. A proper diet for a pet capuchin monkey should reflect this natural variety to ensure that they receive all the essential nutrients required for optimal health.

The primary components of a capuchin monkey's diet include carbohydrates, proteins, fats, vitamins, and minerals. Each of these plays a vital role in their overall health:

- **Carbohydrates** provide the necessary energy for their active lifestyle. Fruits and vegetables are the main sources of carbs in a capuchin's diet.

- **Proteins** are crucial for muscle development, immune function, and overall growth. A healthy capuchin monkey's diet should include protein from both animal and plant-based sources.

- **Fats** are another essential energy source. Healthy fats support skin, coat, and brain health, and also help in the absorption of certain vitamins.

- **Vitamins and minerals** are required for various bodily functions, including immune health, bone health, and tissue repair. These nutrients are generally found in fresh fruits, vegetables, and other whole foods.

Capuchins are active, agile creatures that engage in daily climbing, foraging, and exploring, and their diet must provide the energy needed to fuel these activities. An adequate balance of nutrients is key to keeping them physically and mentally stimulated. Capuchins also rely on their diet for proper digestion and metabolic function, so their meals must be both well-rounded and high in quality.

Safe Fruits, Vegetables, Proteins, and Supplements

Providing a variety of fresh, healthy foods is essential for capuchin monkeys. These foods should be balanced and designed to mimic their natural diet, with appropriate fruits, vegetables, and proteins. Below are the safe and nutritious options for each of these food categories, as well as supplements that can help ensure that your monkey is receiving all necessary nutrients.

Fruits: Capuchin monkeys enjoy a wide range of fruits, which are a rich source of natural sugars, fiber, and vitamins. Some of the best fruits for capuchins include:

- Apples (without seeds)

- Bananas (in moderation)

- Berries (strawberries, blueberries, raspberries)

- Grapes (in moderation)

- Mangoes

- Papayas

- Watermelon

- Pears

It is important to offer fruits that are not overly ripe, as they contain high amounts of sugar, which may contribute to obesity or dental issues in the long term. Variety is key, as each fruit provides a unique set of vitamins and minerals.

Vegetables: Vegetables should make up a significant portion of a capuchin's diet, offering a broad spectrum of vitamins, fiber, and antioxidants. Suitable vegetables include:

- Leafy greens (kale, spinach, lettuce)

- Carrots (preferably raw)

- Bell peppers (red, yellow, or green)

- Cucumbers

- Sweet potatoes

- Zucchini

- Broccoli

While vegetables are an essential part of a capuchin's diet, avoid offering vegetables high in oxalates, such as spinach, in large quantities, as they can interfere with calcium absorption. Leafy greens, in particular, should be fresh and washed thoroughly before feeding to remove pesticides or contaminants.

Proteins: Capuchins require a balanced source of protein for muscle development, immune function, and growth. Protein sources can be both animal-based and plant-based:

- **Animal-based proteins:** These include cooked eggs, small pieces of lean meats (chicken, turkey), or insects such as mealworms and crickets. Wild capuchins often forage for insects, small reptiles, and eggs, making these a more natural source of protein. However, protein from meat should be offered in moderation to avoid excessive fat intake.

- **Plant-based proteins:** Tofu, beans (such as black beans or kidney beans), and legumes are good plant-based protein options. These can be particularly beneficial for capuchins who may not consume animal proteins frequently. Ensure beans are thoroughly cooked, as raw beans can be harmful to monkeys.

Supplements: While a well-balanced diet can generally meet a capuchin's nutritional needs, supplements can sometimes help fill any gaps in their diet. Common supplements for capuchins include:

- **Calcium and Vitamin D**: These are essential for bone health and are particularly important for younger capuchins, who are still growing. You can offer supplements or provide natural sources like kale, collard greens, and fortified foods.

- **Multivitamins**: A high-quality multivitamin supplement designed for primates can help ensure that capuchins are receiving all the necessary vitamins and minerals, especially if their diet lacks variety.

- **Probiotics**: Probiotics can support gut health and help in digestion. If your capuchin has digestive issues, consider offering a probiotic supplement.

Avoiding Toxic Foods and Nutritional Imbalances

While offering a variety of foods to your capuchin is essential, it is equally important to be aware of foods that could be toxic or cause nutritional imbalances. Some foods that are safe for humans and other pets can be harmful or even fatal to capuchins, so always avoid the following:

Toxic Foods to Avoid:

- **Chocolate and caffeine:** These substances contain theobromine and caffeine, which are highly toxic to monkeys and can lead to seizures, heart failure, and death.

- **Avocados:** While avocado is a healthy food for many animals, it contains a substance called persin that can be toxic to monkeys. It can cause heart and respiratory issues.

- **Alcohol:** Just like chocolate and caffeine, alcohol is highly toxic to monkeys and can lead to serious health complications, including liver damage and even death.

- **Nuts:** Some types of nuts, especially salted or roasted nuts, should be avoided. Salted nuts can contribute to sodium toxicity, and the high-fat content can lead to obesity. Raw nuts can also be a choking hazard.

- **Citrus fruits:** While small amounts of citrus fruits are not inherently dangerous, they should be avoided in large quantities. The acidity can upset a capuchin's stomach and potentially cause ulcers.

Nutritional Imbalances:

It is crucial to maintain a balanced diet for your capuchin to avoid nutritional deficiencies or excesses. For instance, a diet too high in fruits can lead to obesity and high blood sugar levels, as fruits are high in natural sugars. On the other hand, a diet with insufficient fat can result in poor coat condition and low energy levels.

A common imbalance seen in pet monkeys is an excess of protein. While protein is important, too much can lead to kidney strain and other health issues. Therefore, it is vital to provide a proper balance between fruits, vegetables, proteins, and fats.

It is also essential to ensure your capuchin gets sufficient calcium in relation to phosphorus to promote healthy bone development. Imbalances between these minerals can lead to bone disorders, such as rickets. Offering calcium-rich foods like leafy greens and fortified food products can help, as long as phosphorus intake is kept in check.

Overall, feeding and nutrition are critical aspects of caring for a capuchin monkey. By understanding their dietary needs and providing a balanced mix of safe fruits, vegetables, proteins, and supplements, you can ensure that your capuchin stays healthy, active, and well-nourished. Always be vigilant about avoiding toxic foods and managing nutritional imbalances to ensure the long-term well-being of your pet. Providing a proper diet not only promotes physical health but also supports mental stimulation, which is vital for the intelligence and emotional balance of a capuchin monkey.

CHAPTER SIX

BONDING AND SOCIALIZING WITH YOUR CAPUCHIN

Capuchin monkeys are highly social, intelligent creatures, known for their curiosity and complex social structures in the wild. As a pet, they require consistent interaction, bonding, and socialization to thrive. Establishing a positive relationship with your capuchin is crucial not only for their emotional well-being but also for ensuring they are well-adjusted to their home environment. This process involves building trust, setting clear boundaries, and employing effective handling techniques. Understanding how to properly interact with your capuchin and integrate them with other pets or humans is essential to forming a deep bond and ensuring a harmonious household.

Building Trust and Establishing Boundaries

Trust is the foundation of any relationship with a capuchin monkey. Unlike many domesticated pets, capuchins are wild animals at their core, and they require time and patience to build trust with their human caregivers. It's important to approach the process with respect and an understanding of their natural instincts and behaviors.

Trust-building begins with consistency and predictability. Capuchins are creatures of habit and feel more secure when their daily routines are consistent. Regular feeding times, safe handling, and a predictable environment help them feel at ease. It's important to interact with your capuchin in a calm, gentle manner and avoid sudden movements or loud noises that could startle them.

Equally important is establishing clear boundaries. Capuchins are intelligent and often curious, and they will explore and test their environment, including their human caregivers. Setting boundaries early on, such as when and where they are allowed to interact with certain objects or areas in the house, helps them understand what is acceptable behavior and what is not. This can be done through gentle redirection, vocal cues, or simple hand signals.

In the early stages of bonding, avoid overwhelming your capuchin with too much attention or too many new experiences. Give them space to adjust to their new environment, especially if they are a rescue or have been recently relocated. As they become more comfortable with you, you can gradually increase the amount of interaction, but always remain aware of their comfort level and never force physical contact.

Handling Techniques and Positive Reinforcement

Proper handling is essential to establishing trust and ensuring your capuchin monkey remains comfortable with human interaction. Capuchins are strong and agile, and improper handling can lead to fear or aggression, both of which can hinder the bonding process.

When handling your capuchin, it's important to approach them slowly and gently. Sudden movements can be perceived as a threat, so try to maintain calm, slow actions. Start with short interactions, such as offering food from your hand or gently petting them, and gradually work your way to longer periods of physical contact. Always be mindful of their body language, as capuchins may communicate discomfort or stress through subtle signs such as stiffening, averting gaze, or vocalizing. If your capuchin shows signs of stress or discomfort, stop the interaction and give them space.

Positive reinforcement is a powerful tool in training and socializing your capuchin monkey. By using treats, praise, and affection as rewards for desired behaviors, you can encourage your capuchin to repeat these actions. For example, rewarding them when they approach you calmly, stay in one place, or perform specific tasks reinforces good behavior and strengthens your bond. It's essential that the rewards are given immediately after the desired action, as this will help your capuchin understand the connection between their behavior and the reward.

Additionally, incorporating training into your daily interactions can help with both bonding and behavior management. Simple commands such as "sit," "stay," or "come" can help develop communication between you and your capuchin. Keep training sessions short and positive, as capuchins can become bored or frustrated with lengthy sessions. Training should always be enjoyable and stress-free for the animal, so remember to remain patient and positive during the process.

Integrating Capuchins with Other Pets or Humans

Socializing your capuchin with other pets and humans is an essential part of their overall well-being. Capuchins are highly social monkeys and generally enjoy the company of others, whether it's another monkey or other animals, provided the introductions are done carefully and respectfully. However, because they are primates, they may not always get along with all pets, especially small animals like birds, rodents, or even cats and dogs.

If you plan to integrate your capuchin with other pets, it is crucial to do so gradually and under supervision. The first step is to allow them to observe each other from a safe distance, giving both animals time to acclimate to each other's presence. Positive reinforcement can be used to encourage calm behavior when your capuchin and the other pet are in proximity. Gradually, under close supervision, you can allow more direct interaction, always watching for any signs of aggression or discomfort from either animal.

When introducing your capuchin to other humans, whether in your household or outside of it, it's important to start slowly. Capuchins are territorial by nature and may feel threatened by unfamiliar people, especially in the early stages of bonding with you. Allow your capuchin to observe newcomers from a distance before any physical interaction takes place. Let the capuchin approach the new person on their own terms. If the capuchin shows interest and exhibits calm behavior, positive reinforcement can be used to encourage further interaction.

Capuchins also form strong emotional bonds with their human caregivers. The more consistent and positive interactions they have with you, the more they will feel secure and trusting. If you have young children in the household, extra care should be taken to supervise all interactions between the capuchin and the children. Children can be unintentionally rough or loud, which can frighten or stress the monkey. It's essential to teach children how to interact with the capuchin in a calm and gentle manner, emphasizing the importance of respecting the animal's boundaries.

It's also important to consider the social needs of your capuchin. While they can bond deeply with humans, capuchins are social animals by nature and may benefit from having a companion, especially if you are away from home frequently. If you are considering getting a second capuchin or other pet to keep your monkey company, be sure to carefully research the species and the process of introducing the animals. Even with proper introductions, not all animals will get along, and it's vital to ensure the safety of both pets.

In summary, Bonding and socializing with your capuchin monkey is a rewarding but gradual process that requires patience, understanding, and consistency. Building trust and establishing boundaries are the first steps in creating a lasting bond, followed by gentle handling and positive reinforcement to encourage desired behaviors. Proper socialization with other pets and humans can help your capuchin live a well-rounded and happy life. By taking the time to nurture a positive relationship, you are ensuring that your capuchin monkey will not only be a beloved companion but also a well-adjusted and content member of your family.

CHAPTER SEVEN

TRAINING AND ENRICHMENT

Training and enrichment are essential for the well-being of capuchin monkeys, as they are highly intelligent, curious, and social animals. Without proper mental stimulation, capuchins can develop behavioral problems, become bored, or even exhibit destructive tendencies. Proper training not only enhances the bond between you and your capuchin but also helps create a more harmonious environment for both pet and owner. Enrichment activities ensure that their cognitive, physical, and social needs are met. By incorporating a variety of training techniques and engaging activities into their daily routine, you can help your capuchin thrive, both mentally and physically.

Teaching Basic Commands and Behavioral Skills

Training your capuchin monkey to follow basic commands and exhibit desired behaviors is an important part of their care. Capuchins are incredibly intelligent, and with patience and consistency, they can learn a variety of behaviors and tricks. Teaching basic commands, such as "sit," "stay," "come," or "no," is not only helpful for daily interactions but also fosters good behavior and creates structure in their lives. The key to successful training is consistency, repetition, and positive reinforcement.

Capuchins respond well to positive reinforcement, such as treats, praise, or affection, when they successfully perform a task. It's crucial to immediately reward the behavior you want to reinforce so that your capuchin associates the action with the reward. Start with simple commands, using clear and concise language, and make sure to reward them promptly after they execute the command. Keep training sessions short—no more than 10 to 15 minutes at a time—since capuchins can lose focus if the sessions are too long. Gradually increase the complexity of the tasks, breaking them down into smaller steps if necessary, to ensure your capuchin remains engaged and motivated.

One important aspect of training is the use of a clicker, a device that makes a distinct sound when pressed. The clicker is used to mark the exact moment a capuchin performs the correct behavior. This helps to quickly communicate to the animal that they did the right thing, which speeds up the learning process. Over time, you can phase out the clicker and rely on verbal commands and rewards alone.

Training your capuchin also includes teaching them to respect boundaries and limits. For example, if your capuchin engages in undesirable behaviors like biting or scratching, it's important to address these behaviors promptly. This can be done using redirection (e.g., giving them a toy to focus on instead of biting) or by using a firm, calm "no" followed by removing them from the situation. Establishing boundaries helps to prevent unwanted behaviors and teaches your capuchin to interact with the environment in a more positive way.

Providing Mental Stimulation Through Games

Capuchin monkeys are natural problem-solvers, and providing them with activities that challenge their cognitive abilities is crucial to preventing boredom and promoting healthy mental development. Mental stimulation can be achieved through interactive games, puzzle toys, and problem-solving activities that encourage your capuchin to think and use their intelligence.

One popular game for capuchins is hiding food in puzzle toys or scattered in various locations within their enclosure. These toys require the monkey to manipulate or figure out how to access the food, which mimics natural foraging behaviors and provides an outlet for their curiosity. Offering a variety of toys with different levels of complexity can help keep their minds engaged. Some toys may require your capuchin to twist, pull, or push objects to reveal hidden treats, and others might involve simple problem-solving exercises.

Interactive games such as "hide and seek" or "fetch" can also help engage your capuchin. These games not only provide physical exercise but also promote mental stimulation as the monkey must figure out how to play the game. For example, you might hide in one part of the house and call out to your capuchin, encouraging them to find you. You could also throw a toy for them to fetch and return, which can become more complex by adding obstacles or multiple toys to collect.

In addition to toys and games, training sessions can be considered part of mental stimulation. Learning new tricks or commands requires the monkey to focus and process information. Varying the types of challenges you present to your capuchin—whether they involve food, puzzles, or social interaction—helps to prevent them from becoming bored or anxious. A stimulating environment is essential for their mental health and overall happiness.

Capuchins also enjoy social interaction, so games that involve cooperation or interaction with you are especially beneficial. For example, teaching your capuchin to pass objects back and forth, or even playing tug-of-war with a rope, can help strengthen your bond while simultaneously offering both mental and physical stimulation.

Preventing and Managing Behavioral Issues

Capuchin monkeys, like any other pet, can develop behavioral issues if their physical, mental, or emotional needs are not adequately met. Because of their high intelligence and curiosity, capuchins may engage in destructive behaviors such as biting, scratching, or even hoarding objects. These behaviors are often a result of boredom, frustration, or insufficient training. By understanding the root causes of these behaviors, you can take steps to prevent them and help your capuchin manage their emotions in healthy ways.

Preventing behavioral issues begins with a comprehensive enrichment plan that includes mental stimulation, physical exercise, and social interaction. Capuchins require constant engagement to prevent them from becoming bored or developing maladaptive behaviors. If they are left in a monotonous or unstimulating environment, they may resort to destructive behaviors such as chewing on furniture, ripping apart objects, or engaging in excessive vocalizations. A variety of toys, daily training sessions, and supervised playtime can help redirect their energy into more positive outlets.

If your capuchin begins to display unwanted behaviors, it's important to respond promptly and consistently. For instance, if they start biting or scratching, a firm "no" followed by immediate redirection to a more appropriate behavior (such as using a toy) is often effective. Using time-outs as a punishment technique can also work, but it should be done in a way that doesn't cause undue stress to the animal. The goal is to show the capuchin that the undesirable behavior leads to a loss of attention or interaction, while the desired behavior results in positive reinforcement.

Another common behavioral issue in capuchins is the development of territorial or possessive behavior, especially over food, toys, or even humans. This can lead to aggression, such as biting or hoarding, if not addressed. To manage territorial behavior, it's important to establish clear boundaries and maintain a structured routine for feeding and playtime. If multiple capuchins or other pets are involved, it may be necessary to monitor their interactions closely and ensure that each animal has access to their own space and resources. Gradual introductions and consistent supervision will help prevent conflicts.

If behavioral issues persist or become severe, it may be helpful to consult with a professional animal behaviorist or a vet who specializes in primate care. An expert can assess the situation, identify the underlying causes of the behavior, and offer strategies tailored to your specific situation.

CHAPTER EIGHT
HEALTH AND VETERINARY CARE

Capuchin monkeys, a beloved species in both the wild and in captivity, are highly intelligent and active animals that require special attention to their health and well-being. Proper veterinary care is crucial to ensuring these fascinating primates live long, healthy, and fulfilling lives. Capuchins are prone to certain health concerns, need routine veterinary check-ups, and may exhibit behavioral or physical signs of stress, illness, or aging. Understanding these elements will empower owners and caretakers to provide the best care possible.

Common Health Concerns: Diseases, Parasites, and Injuries

Capuchin monkeys are susceptible to various diseases, parasites, and injuries that can affect their overall health and quality of life. Being in close contact with humans and other animals increases their risk for some of these issues.

1. **Diseases:**

- **Respiratory Infections:** Capuchins, like many primates, are prone to respiratory infections, especially when housed in indoor environments or where ventilation is poor. These infections can be viral or bacterial and can lead to severe complications if left untreated. Symptoms include coughing, nasal discharge, wheezing, and difficulty breathing.

- **Herpesvirus:** Capuchin monkeys, like other primates, are susceptible to herpesvirus infections, which can cause ulcers, blisters, and more severe systemic illnesses. Regular veterinary check-ups are essential to detect and manage these conditions early.

- **Gastrointestinal Issues:** Monkeys are omnivores and may sometimes ingest food that leads to gastrointestinal disturbances, such as diarrhea, bloating, or vomiting. These symptoms can be signs of infection, food intolerance, or parasitic infections.

2. **Parasites:**

- **Intestinal Parasites:** Capuchins are prone to various gastrointestinal parasites, including roundworms, hookworms, and Giardia. These parasites can cause symptoms like weight loss, diarrhea, and lethargy. A stool sample analysis by a veterinarian is often necessary to identify the presence of parasites.

- **External Parasites:** Capuchins may also harbor external parasites such as lice, ticks, and mites. These parasites can cause discomfort, skin irritation, and, in severe cases, infections. Regular checks for external parasites and maintaining proper hygiene can help prevent infestations.

3. **Injuries:**

- **Fractures and Sprains:** Capuchin monkeys are highly active and agile, and accidents resulting in fractures or sprains are not uncommon, especially when they are allowed free roam in a home or enclosure. These injuries can occur from falls, rough play, or accidents during exploratory behavior. Careful supervision is essential to prevent injuries, and immediate veterinary care is needed if an injury occurs.

- **Bite Wounds:** Aggressive behavior or territorial disputes with other animals can lead to bite wounds, which may become infected if not properly treated. Capuchins' sharp teeth can cause significant damage, and prompt attention to any wounds is necessary.

Routine Check-Ups and Vaccinations

Routine check-ups are essential to maintaining the health of capuchin monkeys. These visits help detect early signs of illness, monitor ongoing conditions, and provide preventive care. Regular health checks can contribute to a longer lifespan and better quality of life.

1. **Health Assessments:**

    - During routine check-ups, a veterinarian will perform a thorough physical exam, checking for signs of malnutrition, dehydration, skin conditions, and abnormalities in movement. Blood tests may be conducted to monitor liver and kidney function, as well as to check for any underlying infections or conditions.

- **Weight Monitoring:** Since capuchin monkeys are highly active, weight can fluctuate depending on their diet and level of exercise. Overweight monkeys are at risk for heart disease, diabetes, and other metabolic disorders, while underweight monkeys might be suffering from malnutrition or illness.

2. Vaccinations:

- Capuchins may require vaccinations to protect them from diseases that can be transmitted by other animals, especially if they are in contact with domestic pets or other wildlife. The specifics of the vaccination schedule depend on the veterinarian's recommendation, but common vaccines for primates may include:

- **Rabies Vaccine:** Rabies is a fatal viral disease that can be transmitted through bites or saliva. Rabies vaccinations are a standard preventive measure for capuchins in regions where the disease is prevalent.

- **Tetanus Vaccine:** Tetanus can occur from deep puncture wounds caused by sharp objects or during accidents. Vaccination is essential for preventing the development of this deadly disease.

- **Influenza Vaccine:** Capuchins can contract flu viruses from humans or other animals. Some veterinarians may recommend a flu vaccine, especially in areas with a high prevalence of influenza.

3. Dental Health:

- Dental problems, including gum disease and tooth decay, can affect capuchins, especially if they are not provided with appropriate food and chew toys. During check-ups, the veterinarian will examine their teeth and gums. Dental care may include professional cleaning or the treatment of any existing dental conditions.

4. Parasite Prevention:

- Regular deworming treatments may be recommended by a veterinarian to ensure that internal parasites do not affect the capuchin's health. External parasite control can also be managed with monthly treatments or preventive measures, such as flea and tick preventatives.

Recognizing Signs of Stress, Illness, or Aging

Capuchins, like all primates, are sensitive to changes in their environment and health. As highly social and intelligent animals, they can exhibit a range of behavioral and physical symptoms when stressed, ill, or aging. Recognizing these signs early can prevent serious health issues.

1. **Signs of Stress:**

   - **Aggressive Behavior:** Stress in capuchin monkeys often manifests as aggression, either towards other animals or humans. This can include biting, vocalizations, and territorial behavior.

   - **Self-harming or Repetitive Actions:** Some capuchins may engage in self-destructive behaviors such as excessive grooming or pulling at their fur. Repetitive behaviors like pacing or rocking may also indicate anxiety or stress.

- **Reduced Appetite or Weight Loss:** Stress can cause capuchins to lose interest in food, leading to weight loss or poor nutrition. Sudden changes in eating habits should always be monitored by a veterinarian.

2. **Signs of Illness:**

- **Changes in Activity Level:** A sudden decrease in energy, reluctance to move, or excessive sleeping can signal illness. Capuchins are normally active, and any drastic change in behavior should prompt a visit to the vet.

- **Discharge or Unusual Odors:** Any discharge from the eyes, nose, or mouth, or unusual odors from the body, can indicate an underlying infection. These should be addressed by a veterinarian as soon as possible.

- **Difficulty Breathing:** Labored breathing, wheezing, or coughing are signs of respiratory distress, which requires immediate veterinary attention.

3. **Signs of Aging:**

- As capuchins age, they may begin to show signs of arthritis or joint pain. This could manifest as limping, slower movement, or difficulty jumping or climbing, activities that are usually effortless for younger monkeys.

- **Cognitive Decline:** Older capuchins may experience a decline in their cognitive abilities, including memory and problem-solving skills. This can manifest in confusion or changes in behavior.

- **Changes in Coat Quality:** Aging can also affect a capuchin's coat, which may become thinner, drier, or lose its luster. Regular grooming and a proper diet can help maintain coat health, but changes in appearance can be a natural part of aging.

Overall, the health and well-being of a capuchin monkey depend on proper care, routine veterinary check-ups, and an awareness of common health concerns. Owners must stay vigilant for signs of illness, stress, or aging, and take preventive measures, such as vaccinations and parasite control, to ensure the long-term health of their monkeys. With the right care and attention, capuchin monkeys can thrive in captivity, maintaining both their physical health and mental stimulation.

CHAPTER NINE
LONG-TERM CARE AND LIFESTYLE CONSIDERATIONS

Owning a capuchin monkey is a long-term commitment that requires extensive knowledge of their care and a dedication to providing a safe, stimulating, and healthy environment throughout their entire life. As intelligent, social animals, capuchins experience various developmental stages, and understanding these stages can help owners provide the appropriate care as they age. This section explores the lifespan and developmental stages of capuchin monkeys, how to address behavioral changes over time, and the strategies for ensuring a happy and fulfilling life for your capuchin.

Lifespan and Developmental Stages

Capuchin monkeys are known for their longevity, especially when they are provided with proper care in captivity. In the wild, their average lifespan is around 40 years, while in captivity, where they are protected from predators and have access to veterinary care, they can live well into their 50s or even 60s. This extended lifespan makes it all the more important to be prepared for the long-term care requirements of your capuchin, including the mental and physical needs that evolve over time.

Developmental Stages: From infancy to adulthood, capuchins go through several stages of development that influence their care. In their early years, capuchin monkeys are highly dependent on their mothers for both nourishment and social learning. In the first few months of life, they are particularly vulnerable to stress and environmental changes. Infants are curious and playful, but their development during this time is fragile. During this stage, they need extra attention, a carefully balanced diet, and secure bonding with their caregivers.

As capuchins reach adolescence (around 2 to 3 years old), they start to assert their independence. They may become more active and testing of their boundaries. Adolescents often exhibit more complex social behaviors and may demonstrate dominance or attempt to form alliances. During this stage, it's important to continue socialization and training to guide them toward appropriate behaviors and establish clear boundaries.

By the time capuchins reach adulthood (around 5 to 7 years old), they are fully mature both physically and emotionally. Adult capuchins are more predictable in their behaviors and have established their social dynamics, which may involve relationships with humans or other animals. However, they still require daily enrichment and social interaction to avoid boredom and maintain their emotional well-being. At this stage, providing opportunities for mental stimulation and play becomes crucial to keeping them engaged and content.

As capuchins approach their senior years (around 20 years old), their health needs become more pronounced. Like all aging animals, they may begin to experience a decline in physical mobility, a decrease in energy levels, or changes in behavior. Senior capuchins may require a modified diet to accommodate any dental issues or digestive changes, as well as additional veterinary care to monitor their health. It's important to ensure that their living environment is comfortable and safe, with easy access to climbing structures and mental enrichment activities to keep them active within their abilities.

Addressing Behavioral Changes Over Time

As capuchins age, their behavior may change, and it is essential for owners to adapt to these shifts in order to maintain a healthy relationship with their pet and promote their well-being. Behavioral changes can be caused by various factors, including physical health issues, changes in social dynamics, or aging-related conditions.

Behavioral Shifts in Adolescence and Adulthood: During adolescence, capuchins may exhibit an increase in independence and may become more territorial or display behaviors associated with sexual maturity. This is the period when capuchins often test their limits with their human caregivers, which can result in undesirable behaviors like biting or tantrums if not addressed properly. It is crucial to maintain consistency in training during this stage, offering positive reinforcement when your capuchin exhibits desired behaviors and gently correcting undesirable ones.

In adulthood, capuchins typically settle into a more predictable routine. They often have a well-established social structure and may begin to form stronger bonds with humans or other animals in the household. While they may become more affectionate and easier to handle, their need for mental stimulation remains high. Failure to provide regular enrichment or a change in their environment can lead to boredom, stress, and destructive behaviors.

Behavioral Issues in Senior Capuchins: As capuchins age, certain behavioral changes can occur that require special attention. For example, they may become more lethargic or less interested in activities that previously engaged them. Cognitive decline, like that seen in humans as they age, can also affect capuchins, leading to memory lapses, confusion, or disorientation. It's essential to monitor for signs of dementia or changes in mood and behavior, such as increased aggression, irritability, or a lack of social interest, which may indicate underlying health problems.

Senior capuchins may also exhibit a decline in social interactions, preferring solitude or disengaging from their human caregivers. Providing extra comfort, maintaining a low-stress environment, and adjusting their diet to address physical health concerns can help manage these behavioral shifts. Older capuchins may require more rest and gentle handling, and adjustments to their environment, such as easier access to food and water, can help them maintain comfort as they age.

Ensuring a Happy and Fulfilling Life for Your Capuchin

Creating a happy and fulfilling life for your capuchin monkey involves meeting not only their basic physical needs but also their emotional and social needs. Capuchins are social animals that thrive on interaction, engagement, and mental stimulation. Providing a stimulating environment, consistent social interaction, and ongoing training will go a long way in ensuring your capuchin remains healthy and happy throughout their life.

1. Social Interaction: Capuchins are highly social creatures that, in the wild, live in large groups and rely on complex social structures. In captivity, they may form strong bonds with their human caregivers, but it's important to remember that they still require socialization with others of their species. If possible, providing opportunities for your capuchin to interact with other monkeys or animals can help satisfy their social needs.

Regular interaction with humans is equally important for bonding. Capuchins enjoy human company and can form deep emotional attachments to their caregivers. Consistent positive interactions, such as playing, talking, or training, are crucial to building and maintaining a strong bond. It's also important to spend quality time with your capuchin each day, even if it's simply sitting together or allowing them to explore their environment with supervision.

2. Mental Stimulation: Because of their high intelligence, capuchins need constant mental stimulation. Boredom can lead to behavioral issues like excessive vocalization, self-destructive behaviors, or aggression. Providing mental enrichment through puzzle toys, foraging activities, and training sessions is essential for their well-being. Incorporating variety in their playtime and ensuring they have opportunities to explore their surroundings can help keep them engaged.

3.Diet and Physical Activity: Maintaining a balanced diet and encouraging physical activity are also critical to their long-term health. Regular exercise through climbing structures, toys, and playtime helps to keep them physically fit and emotionally healthy. Their diet should be diverse, providing the necessary nutrients to support their energy levels, skin, and immune system. Special attention should be given to their diet as they age to ensure they receive the right nutrients for their health needs.

4. Regular Veterinary Care: Finally, regular veterinary visits are essential to monitor and maintain your capuchin's health throughout their life. As mentioned earlier, health issues can arise at any stage, and early detection is key to preventing more serious problems. By staying on top of vaccinations, check-ups, and health concerns, you ensure that your capuchin leads a long and healthy life.

By focusing on the individual needs of your capuchin, respecting their natural behaviors, and providing them with a supportive and stimulating environment, you can ensure that they live a happy, fulfilling life, regardless of their age.

CONCLUSION

In conclusion, owning a capuchin monkey is a significant commitment that requires a deep understanding of their unique behavioral, social, and physical needs. These intelligent and social primates thrive in environments that provide mental stimulation, social interaction, and proper care throughout their lifespan. From creating a safe, enriched habitat to ensuring their nutritional and healthcare needs are met, capuchin monkeys demand attention, patience, and consistency. However, with the right preparation and a genuine commitment to their well-being, capuchins can make loyal and engaging companions, offering a fulfilling and rewarding experience for responsible owners.

THANKS FOR READING.

www.ingramcontent.com/pod-product-compliance
Lightning Source LLC
Chambersburg PA
CBHW061246250726